THE LAST DAY *AND* THE FIRST

BOOKS BY THEODORE WEISS

Selections from *The Note-Books
of Gerard Manley Hopkins*
The Catch (Poems, 1951)
Outlanders (Poems, 1960)
Gunsight (A Long Poem, 1962)
The Medium (Poems, 1965)
The Last Day and the First (Poems, 1968)

THE LAST DAY
AND
THE FIRST

Poems by Theodore Weiss

THE MACMILLAN COMPANY, *New York*

COLLIER-MACMILLAN LTD., *London*

ACKNOWLEDGMENTS

Most of the poems in this volume, some of which appear here in revised form, were first published in the following magazines: *Delos*: "A Russian Lesson," "Malady," "Fresh Paint," "Sultry Dawn," "A Poem Recalled," "Inside the Storm," "From A to Z"; *Dryad*: "Wunsch-zettel"; *The Malahat Review*: "A Summer Thundershower" (now "A Summer Thunderstorm"), "Blithewood," "This Gray Age"; *The Nation*: "Robes of the Gods," "Sweet Talk," "The Ultimate Antientropy." The poem "The Life of . . ." appeared originally in *The New Yorker*, © 1967 The New Yorker Magazine, Inc.; "Mount Washington" in *Perspective*; the following in *Poetry*: "The Last Day and the First," "Between the Lines," and "Far Out, Far In"; "Caliban Remembers" and "A Midsummer Nightmare" in *The Quarterly Review of Literature*; "A Letter from the Pygmies" in *The Saturday Review*; "Lines for an Ending" in *Sewanee Review*; "The Eighth Day" and "The Way It Works Out" in *The Yale Review*, Winter 1966, Summer 1968, respectively, copyright Yale University; and "November Late" and "To Anna Akhmátova" in *Voyages*.

Library of Congress Catalog Card Number: 68-23645

FIRST PRINTING

The Macmillan Company, New York
Collier-Macmillan Canada Ltd., Toronto, Ontario

Printed in the United States of America

Contents

THE LAST DAY *AND* THE FIRST

The Last Day and the First

The stocky woman at the door,
with her young daughter "Linda" looking
down, as she pulls out several copies
of *The Watchtower* from her canvas bag,
in a heavy German accent asks me:
"Have you ever thought that these
may be the last days of the world?"

And to my nodding "Yes, I have,"
she and the delicate, blonde girl
without a further word, turning tail,
sheepishly walk away.
                            And I feel
for them, as for us all, this world
in what may be its last days.
And yet this day itself is full
of unbelief, that or marvelously
convincing ignorance.
                            Its young light
O so tentative, those first steps
as of a beginning dance (snowdrops
have already started up, and crocuses
we heard about last night the teller's
children quickly trampled in play)

make it hard not to believe that we are
teetering on creation's brink all over
again. And I almost thrill with fear
to think of what will soon be asked
of us, of you and me;
                            am I at least
not a little old now (like the world)
to be trembling on the edge
of nakedness, a love, as Stendhal

knew it, "as people love for the first
time at nineteen and in Italy"?

Ah well, until I have to crawl
on hands and knees and then can crawl
no more, so may it every Italian-
returning season be, ever the last
day of this world about to burst
and ever for blossoming the first.

CALIBAN REMEMBERS

Caliban Remembers

                              Might
have gone with them. Might. To be—
I heard their scheming—a strange fish,
stranded on land, lurching in shadows,
a monster they, tormenting, make.
No one for me. Not my master's kind
with perfumes stinking, auks at courting.
Nor to me true friends those two
I fell in with.
                    Oh fell in with,
a horse-pond for our pains, and over
ears, scum sticking to, thick scum.

"Putrid fish," all scoffed at me.
As if, from king on down, they did
not take their thrashed turn in the sea.
As in the way they reached this shore.

On such a day—moons marching by
my marking time—sat I out here,
sat, shading me, beneath this cliff.
The sea, one blinding wave, bulged round.
The sun had soaked deep into it,
into each bush, each tree. Had soaked
into these rocks until they shook
with light.
                    There—I fished then too—
a great wind suddenly blowing up,
foam in its mouth, a bloody shriek,
that boat.
                    Again and again surf broke
on it. Yet sparkling everywhere,

a blaze that, sizzling, blazed the more,
boat, gliding over this cove's jag rocks,
rode in. By then, for lightning's rifts,
one wave hot after me the sea,
I scuttled off, got me to
my sty's dark cleft and, glad at last
to have it, hid.
          My rod dangles,
once more sways the waters, swelling
from the line. New shadows come,
noises I hear past what such brooding
high-noon brings. Hummings out of the sea
and the air, out of the woods?
             Long tides
ago, I remember, hardly remember,
there were others. Low voices, rough,
could find me out, prod me, please.
No wasp's bite sharper, whirring through,
no grape-burst sweeter. Vague at best
now, like the name he'd knot to me.

Yet things I have belonged to them.
This gown, a giant ringdove's rainbow-
downy hood, I lounge in, tatters
and all, once my master while at magic
needs must wear, with that rod fishing
outlandish cries, their creatures in them,
from air and sea.
          Lurked among books
he left. At times, efts in heaped leaves
as out of sleep, they pop. Yet as I
bend they fade, day after day
farther away.
          But next to my hand
this pebble, blinked at me, a trinket
it might have been, dropped that time
I stumbled on her dreaming here,
dazzled by her still, as her glass,

cast off, raised to the face, a look
flashing, says she's, passing, teasing,
by behind me.
                    Chalk-faced, hair
sleeked down, no otter's better, stalked
behind her, basking in her light,
so darking me who saw her first,
that Ferdinand.
                    How push back
this crinkle badgers brow?
                    Witch she,
not my poor mother, I tweaked as ever,
as a jay its secretest feather.
And most, blood at the heart hopping,
dare I speak out her name.
                    Sometimes
taste still—remembering billows body
through, delight battering—gust
of that liquor. Cloud-casked surely,
music fermented. Those two bidding me
drink, one gulp, and no more goading
for me. God I, the sky my gliding,
earth, everything in it my subject,
far below.
                    Now, if ever they were,
gone. Even my sleep, only rarely
whispering in it, slips free of them.

From the thicket, peeping, watched
the long ship I helped stow fruit, fish,
water aboard sweep out and silently,
its sails confused with clouds, folding,
unfolding, melt as though the wind,
seeing them go, blew merrily.

At first I also, kicking up heels,
scattered round their garments, linens,
books. At first. But after—find

7

again that whole belonging mine
before they came?—and worst those days
when I, a smoke, fume through my hands,
loneliness whelms me.
                              Had I only
his book's good company, that company
it kept waiting, perfect, on him,
humble the world, I'd lord it truly.

My rod, sprouting though it did
from the staff he thought forever buried
and I plucked it, swish as it will
to rouse the breezes, rustle the sea,
fish shaken out, fat birds, their feathers
fluttered brightly as their cries,
fares forth no revelries like his,
nor no revelations neither.

Times I'd welcome the old, heavy
chores, his orders at roughest irk,
echoed in cramps, nips, pinches,
hedgehogs packed and inchmeal wedging
through me.
                       Times they rack me still,
those pokes, side-stitches (feared at first—
my shivers mounted—he'd returned;
aches he had, all kinds and fit
for each part of the body, aches
he must have stuffed in hollow branches
sealed with pitch and as the music
from his pipe, as smoke behuffed
into the breath, at will puffed out);
and shapes they do in the dark, giddily
torching me that I slubber in bogs,
on mad bushes burr me, furzes clawing.
But now with no sense of meaning, no ape-
mouthing sprites behind them to mock,
not anger, only themselves.

8

Themselves
those plumes awag at the water's edge,
draggled through mire, flood, yet dry,
a play straight out of the spume?
Not those
from the ship again, untouched, a miracle,
unless the shine they sport be sea's
(my master bragged he kept them so),
nor straggle-heeled in memory,
but a dirt-glittering file, great bugs.

Well, what comes, more or less, I accept,
my state on the isle. Its flocks and herds,
its slyest creatures, these, as I pluck
for hides, food, feathers, tribute
also in their squawky cowering,
at least acknowledge me King. Tame too
as they never were for those. Long days
I loll, ruler and subjects the same.

Things I learned, it is true, some,
nag at me still, names that, shimmering,
as I would clamp jaws to, dissolve.
And the faces glimmered out at me
from bush and sky, tide-riding shapes.

Came on her in this very cove,
swimming still on her, whiter, rounder
than a wave dashed on the shore,
drops drying like pearls, open to the sun.
Then I understood his daily command:
"Stand upright, stand!" Upright I was,
knew at last what he meant by "Be
a man." Saw she was gone there, torn
out by the roots. Wish in sudden,
flushed kindness, pity, give her mine,
all.
But tiptoed, manhood in hand,

to surprise her, completed while she slept,
as by magic—was it our fires,
crossing, drew him?—scepter quivering,
upright, he appears. Eyes blazed
on me, cares, it seems, nothing
I have learned my lesson, prompt
to obey.
            Fear he had I'd fish
his pond? Oh no, not fish it, stock it!
Who else was there to do her turn,
so save the day for man on the island?
Not all his magic, age, can angle
new foundlings, me more, out of air.
Mere thinking it wrings.
                Still his words,
crackling, strike me everywhere stony
if feelingful. One frown farther
I had been done.

II

But hear that hiss.

Its skin atwitch, the sea would speak?
A rumbling scrabbles.
             And the rod
grows taut, throbs, humming, in my hands.
Some odd, mad fish I've caught? Haul
it up.
       There, soaked, dripping,
thick sighs spluttered from it, bobs
a swollen, slippery thing.
                Clutch it.
A book. That book? My master's prize,
the one he wished drowned!
               Alive again;
inside its blotched pages, sea sick,
for all the sights, outlandish worlds,
it's gulped, the words, through fingers slither-
ing minnows, hop. Mixed in its spells now,

nymphs he cropped, nymphs and urchins,
romping, couple, splotched with purple
swirling.
          Clouds he called this world,
clouds and dreams (a sorcerer then,
a stronger, over him, mouthing things,
wording us, puffed thus into being,
browsing on our aches and rages?).
Such waking cloud this book's become.
Reading—fidgety gnat-words, flicking
eye—not hard enough!
                    Yet some,
their tails, flouncing, all I catch
as if plunged, the rest of them,
twinkling, into the sea or swamped
by smudgy ink, I nearly recognize.

Put ear to page, hear something, grumbling
steady, a power, far off, collecting.
His voice, is it, penned in the words?

This the book, the very one
he used, depended on most, most
to abuse me.
            Master he may have been,
yet could do nothing without me. Not,
unless I, fetching sticks, patched fire,
rouse his magic, its highflown tricks.
Whatever his flights, had to return
to this island, his cell, me.
Never could, whatever his flights,
go back to his country till they came
with that ship. I only propped him, kept
as earth does sky, else dropped in the sea.

Why then should I not use it also?
Shake me out music, that brave host,
showering praises, presents isle-heaped:

luscious fruits flung from the trees;
liquors clouds, cask-big, split,
pour down, thirsty for my tongue;
fish pied flying in out of waves
as the sea itself, glistening, bows,
then at my feet stows dutiful ships,
with treasure crammed as giant hives,
their honeycombs oozing.
                              Maybe can,
why not, raise one fair as she,
a dozen, sea-blooms, wreathing her,
bent on one thing only, hooked,
dolphin-sleek, dished in the sun,
one thing: pleasing me.
                              Cloudy as sky,
bow-taut, is growing, better hurry.
Drape the robes about me, so.
Wagging the staff, take that half-
crouched, half-stiff stance, nose aloft
as though snuffling powerful scents,
the music working under things.

Now find the place in the book.
                              Here,
the lines most faded. Head nodding
right, then left, both eyes rolling,
yet lordly, words begin to twist.

And body caught in the sway, they sound
something like this.
                              (Never knew,
clever as he believed he was,
often through a chink I spied
on him mumbo-jumboing to air,
then jutting ear as if he thought
to hear answer. And was there something,
mutters, say the air's bright crest,

12

aflutter, speaking, speaking I
now seem to be hearing out of these
drowsy trees?)
     Oh, could he see
me now, his lessons like his scepter
clutched, the earth, the sea, the cloud-
packed sky about to wake, how pleased
he'd have to be.
     I can, mouth gulped,
almost repeat that rounded phrase
finished off in a hiss.
     Lo, now, lo!
Even as I say it, darkness hedges,
crowding out of the sea.
     Beware!
A lightning crashes, fire's scribble
scratchy down sky; and that oak, sky-tall,
falls at my feet.
     Homage truly.
One twig closer and I had been ever
more crowned!
     Wake that squall again?
Watching him manage it, hearing
out of it bellows, no beasts madder,
demons not (suppose more loosed
than he could handle?), shuddered me
through.
     There, high on its ruff, the osprey
its spray, the cormorant beaking it,
muscular mist, and riding, gay
as a porpoise, a gull, in the distance
the ship bobbing that took them off!

Desire that: my master back,
she, the others, logs, fast rooted
where I dumped them, ache in my bones,

the play, I ever cast for monster,
slave, to be played over and over?

Oh no. Now this able book's mine,
my lackeys they.
                              Ah the sweet tasks
I'd conjure up for them as—standing,
upright, rigid, by, they glare
their envy's deadly looks—I lie
in my flower-soft bed, she, flower
among flowers, by me, mistress
to my least worded, far-fetched whim,
breath mixed with, winging, lilac, thyme.

And him I bid bring turtle eggs,
struggle through fanged briers for berries,
prickles too of bees he must snatch
choicest honeysacks from.
                              The others,
husked of rapiers, ruffs, fine airs,
down on all fours, the beasts they are,
cuff them, kick. Out of their yelping,
as master's pipe could ply a storm,
pluck music.
                    One bears me a bowl
brims rose-water, petals swimming;
and dabbling hands, on another I wipe.
Then order these pour ripest wine
down throat. Or "Scratch the regal back
with porcupine." Set on the palace
his book shows, "Scoop out that fen.
Put rocks over there. There. And there."
And, put, not liking it, "Put back
again."
            But as they, drooping, sigh,
their struts and frets, wildfire plots,
gone out, would I not let them be,

14

him most, most haggard for these labors
far beyond his years, and he, first
landing on this shore, enjoying
for a time what he found here, most kind?
As I enjoyed, a time, the silks,
the warmth and airs he (she more) soothed
against me.
         Best in the twilit cool,
as now, puffed from the earth and sea,
the shadows out of the deepening wood.
Then, he piping, I sprawled by,
the notes bubbling, dewy moonlight
vibrant on them, as in her eyes
glittering secrets of caves sea-kept,
she sang. And winds and waves, chins set
in their hands, the stars, leant down, peering
ever harder as darkness ripened,
also sang. One radiant sound,
the earth and sky involved in it,
soaked into me, I shook with light.

So he, sitting over me—great patience
he had, as I at my fishing—listened.
Points at things, making fish mouths,
stranger noises. And a mote
baiting my eye, a may-fly twirling,
whole day, if tiny, on midnoon,
prods with "Mind, mind!" till at last,
no salmon swifter thrashing waters,
flipped above the spray, the word,
in me erupting, pops from my lips.

Joy in him then, love like my own.
Eager to show me this thing, that,
bold for the blessing of a name.
Tales he unfolds with airs in them
from castles as from clouds that dances

gleam like waterfalls, beteeming
stately woods, by birds set off.
His books spread out before me, shared,
I learn to pin their swart bugs down.

A book, it seems, for everything,
for things that cannot be and never
could. Had one even showing me
and called, so it said, "Caliban"
because I fed, not less gladly
than on ants, on men. How could I,
no man being here? And think
of eating those, washed up, rotten,
worse than flotsam, on this shore!
To them alone such name belongs
who would, not cold, not hungry, kill.
(The name I had I never told,
with mother buried who gave it me.)

But best of all that warbling book,
written as on a cloud, about clouds,
the world so graved, growing, changing,
one thing into another, like a cloud,
its women turning, as the pages
do, into a tree, a brook,
a song. Who would have thought, with nothing
left of them, their silvery looks,
their voices, but the sighing of a leaf,
a rivulet, the hearer's tears
jet forth, the world seen newly
in their light.
                    But am not I,
not merely stone, such changeling too?
So she, in one day sped from childhood
stalk-thin, awkward, into woman.
What I became she could not see
but only heard, as I would sigh,

the same old shaggy husk of me,
as that god, changed, so the book said,
into a bull for love, must bellow.

Books browsed on as my own. All,
that is, but one and that craved most.
No matter how I strained, heaven
it loomed, mocking, over my head.
And that the book I saw him lost
in, sitting by the fire, listening
to its gossip, mixed with the jiggly
words, his stare outgleaming embers.
That tongue, so good at wagging, flogging,
little about him then but as it
jogs off on its own. And the eye
that easily caught me out, no eye
for me, a thing that never was.

Mornings too, quick to me earth,
the berries restless in their plot,
the sky as well, I know it time
to tend the day. And he shut away
as though, beyond those pages marked,
no light, no joy, can bloom.
                              Damned be
such book when world in lark enough,
in filbert and in plum, cries out
that I become a winged hearing,
lapping tongue, and those the ground-
work eyes and hands abound them in,
my feelings, ripened as they ripe.

Let him be buried in his glimmering
dark while I sprawl in the sun,
in busy, slow pleasure running hot
fingers over me. Or, plunging,
lounge inside the thicket, tickled

by the shade, webs buzzing, leaf-mold
rotting on mold, a wood-bug sometimes
gulped with a berry.
                    Long hours on
and into the night within my fingers,
under my lids, the daylight tingles,
tingle too along my dreams
those sizzling smells, the fruits as when
I munched on them. And he, after,
the fire gone out? Gray, ash-gray.

Yet that one book—now I have it!—
is it better than the world, telling
where winds are woven, snows, sundowns,
showing them being made, and played
out as its owner bids?
                    Some god
must have bestowed it on my master,
else dropped it—as later he did—
lying open, wind-leafed, wind-sighing,
like this earth, and my master found it.

Time and place forgot, he wandered
in it, blissfully lost, the world
assorted, cherries, rainbows, beetles
boxed. So on this island all
the seasons at once or, as he wished,
seasons of most outlandish countries,
mountains in his cell and light
as clouds, tall mountains flaming round
the embers, goddesses too and sprites—
the show of them.
                    But then he saw—
perhaps the days between the spells,
their willingness to work, grew longer,
harder, or he woke, ash-gray—
what empty dream he'd snared him in,

18

learned the lesson I had always known:
with that book to give himself, to dive
into the thrilling waters, chilled
at times, hard buffeting, this world,
this life is?
                    Maybe, come back, stroking
and teaching again, his words mine,
I finding some he did not know
like new nests, crag-set, I could show
him, eggs speckled with writing brighter
than his book's, sly birds, the topmost
sky still breathing from their wings,
in their songs still, he'd once more trust,
entrust the isle, his rule, as mate
his daughter.
                    May that ribboned thing,
filched my place with the logs, her fancy
also, drown, this time for good,
a delicate food lining fish bellies,
sweet between my royal teeth.
Then, who knows, she might, seeing
him at last so much in me,
like me the more.
                    Or, better, let him,
soaked enough, grown scaly through
and through, yanked out, Caliban me.
If he, pale sprout, could supplant me,
why I not him? Three times as much
as his dragged, staggering poor armful,
he a king's son, I can haul.

Our names with their three syllables,
two mountains humping a crouched "i"—
Cal-i-ban and Ferd-i-nand,
Ferdinand and Caliban—
are surely like enough so that
the mouth which shaped out his with loving

breath, trill birds would stop to hear,
to mine could be as kissing-kind?
Ah, well, would she ever have—
how could she—loved a thing like me?

Why, instead of all that work,
those lessons, slow, dull, scratchy,
did my master, worlds at hand,
not turn me presto into prince?
Sea, fire, sky he managed
featly; but I too much for him,
earth magic alone could never change?

Never, as he sought to stuff me
with his learning, asked he me
my thought, my feeling. All I was
was wrong, to change. All he wished
was aping, my face wrought to look,
a mirror, more and more like his.

III

The book in hand, past teaching now.
Let's see, squatting under this rock,
what rubbing these, the last two words,
together does.
                    That grating stink,
dredged up from grotto bottoms, bogs,
sunk under the sea.
                    And swelling out,
choking the air, one racketing cry.

He's back, overseeing me, making me
do what I do. Or Setebos
with his accursed crew, sneaked in
at last and most to devil me—
who else is left to feed their hate?—
for being driven off.

                    A crack
as though the earth is splitting!
                              Out there,
lit, the ocean spouts. One monstrous
fish?
        No, upright, like a mighty
man in flashing robes and roars—
if only he came back how gladly
I would give this book, myself,
and all the isle to him once more—
I see it, see his city, so he
called it, climbing the skies, its spires,
cloud-piled, the gardens sauntering
with gilded fountains, songs torch-lit,
while far below dark fires rage,
the swamp on which such city's built.

Like torrents crashing over a crag
it burrows every secret store
of me, one shattered ear.
                        Now crumbles,
tumbling drags the outermost rim
of the isle with it!
                    My doing? Not done
a lone thing yet brings me one crumb
of joy; no music—only this howling,
sky clipt open, trolls my name.

What if, the salt marsh flushed and pounced
on me, I move the moon, the sea
rushed over the isle, I among mollusks
down there, for sharks a crunchy music?

Ass enough that time I dreamed
I could, with those two clumsy sots,
set me free, get rule. Master
I called one, god, licking his foot,
and he, for all the sack in him,

not mire good enough to cake
my master's boot. And I believed
he'd bottled moonshine, music, himself,
the moon's own man, dropped with them!

Oh lessoned I am. Off with the gown
and break the wand. Before this book,
more than ever my master did,
reigns over me, ruins entirely,
drown it again. Never wanted it
in the first place.
                              So let it sink.
Dissolved into the restlessly paging
(seems to be reading it), gurgling sea,
the nymphs and dolphins schooled by it,
it may, sea-changed, sigh out its message.
As now.
                    Whatever his tempest brought
about, this one washes me clean
of them, blundering on their tottery
two feet (upright they pride themselves
on being!), in broad daylight bethicketed,
wilder than night. And all the time
planning havoc.
                    Why so foolish
as to toss his power away and, naked,
return to a world bustling with men,
his brother, my silly crew, repeated
a thousand, thousand times over? Expose,
as well as himself, his dear daughter
to infections, plagues, far past the wiles
of scummy ponds!
                    Devils they said
haunting this island. No least devil
till they arrived. Not all the toads
and frogs this island spawns could quell
the viper in them. Devils he sailed

away with, devils, waiting, hordes,
to dog him all his life's last days.
Think of a world, an island like this,
swarmed with them, their schemings, brawls!

Winds blow over me, the crooning
night air, free now, full of nothing
but its own breath, serenades
the locusts chirr, scents of the sea
and this my island, twining with
what stars are pouring.
                         Yet, not burrs
snarled tighter in the hair, they cling,
that manyed voice, as in a sea-
shell, ebbing, wailing, far inside
into my ear.
                    Fingers remember
the bowl they brought, his hand on it,
hers, the water gushed forth, sparkling,
laughter, words. I polishing,
how it gleamed in pleasure, over-
wrought with my face.
                         Its carvings music
swelling to the eye, the finger,
from the pipe the piper on it
raises who is blowing out
the rounded, cloud-big, smoky sky,
I enter it, the little landscape
centered in thick trees a wind
in fragrant waves is wreathing, wreathing
me, shapes watching.
                         Him I see,
see her approaching. Eyes smart,
fingers tingle, taught sly snaggings
of silk, as eyes are caught by her
skirt rustling, the drop of her lids
a deafening tide in the blood till I,

battered as by that liquor's gust,
for the flooding over me drown.

Oh no, not that again, not me
gone in the dark of too much light.
Not bowls, nor touching words, to push
me out of me.
                    There, smash it
to the earth, the dust it after all
is. And through its shattered pieces,
him and her, those others scattered,
I tramp free, free as the air.

But free of what? Not lost, all ebbed
away, as water from the bowl,
for that they would have taught?
                              Too high
he rose, high-handed reached past earth
into the clouds he sacked, while I
          , an earth, below.
                    At last
he changed his mind, chose man, the life
that all men lead, a magic, dream
more than enough?
                    Preferred the bowl
no less at breaking, robes faded
and faces, dyings, their plots too,
their hates.
          But most that momentary,
everlasting human touch—to touch
Miranda's hand again! A queen now,
joy of children throning her
as they, shrill, ruckle round her knees?
And he, does he live still, sometimes,
head shaking, bent in some forgotten
corner over an old book,
muttering maybe "Caliban"?—

24

the fearful, wide-open risk of it,
feeling, as men feel, as men call it
real.
      Preferred. As I finally learned,
little though he knew it, learned
to love him, going. And do.
                    No matter
how I burrow in shadows on shadows,
leaves thick and dark mixing, dark
from inside owl wings, bat's screechy
darting, my cave sealed off, I stick out,
prickly, listening.
          How I long
to hear once more those me-completing
voices. Come back, would cast me
at their feet. And yet . . . alone, alone
as he must be, loathing, pitying, loving.

BY REASON OF DARKNESS

The Eighth Day

Twilight lidding the fifth day,
did He steep His hands in them, self-
reaping riches newly won, His powers
proud to see themselves adorned
by what they did—
             the horned, lowing
as they moved, a forest headlong,
into balmy slumber like His stabling
hands: the serpents, no more twisted
than their manes: the condors,
                 bedded
in their puffed-up feathers, curling
by the lambs, with vines festooning,
consummating dark: winds also, water,
nodding to their hum?
             And still
the coursing in His fingers of that
thoroughfare, the lovely and com-
mingled traffic burst from Him, stars
too dazzled
          in that all-talking air.
Having made so much, each a witness
to His growing mastery, sufficient
to itself if not to Him, He must
pass on,
        press through these others
to the last, the one in whom the rest
would congregate, who, gisted of them,
would at once be able to salute
the thoroughfare
           with names that,
murmuring, afford them room to mine
and bruit their teeming, secret wealth.
Accordingly, this sixth day, upright,
strove to be,

the manly day that,
harking back through bird and snake,
tree, water, star and wind, would feel
these words, those hands, so resonant
within he must break free.

A Letter from the Pygmies

Dear Whoever-You-Are-That-You-Are,

Whatever chance this has of reaching You,
I write to bring You up to date.

I cannot, little as I join them
in their skills at hunting,
undertake Your tigers. Rarely
do Your lofty auks invite me
to the confabs of their aeries.
Pastimes Leviathan delights in
never has he offered to share
with me; never has he proffered
island back or cove-snug belly.

Still there is the cat Hoppy
who, whatever our blandishments,
as he cannot drop his creaturehood,
claws flying in his pleasure, takes me
some good distance into Your creation;
dew starlit on his fur, the fields
wherein Your wonders grow he smells of.
And when, unblinkingly, he fixes me
as though he were upon the scent

of rabbit, mouse, or other friend,
I know the instantaneous delight
of terror. So elation finds me
in the chickadee that bobs
upon our thrashing window-bush,
skullcap awry like any plucky Jew's,
a Job in synagogue of ashes, cries;
as Hoppy bats the pane, it never
budges from our fat-packed rind.

31

In short, though there's a scheme
afoot to blow Your ark and all in it
to smithereens, to pitch a cloudy,
climbing tower will convert the earth
into one tomb, I know by feelings
craning, preening deep inside
the ark's still riding, riding high.

So from time to time, what time remains,
I'll do my best to keep in touch with You.

Faithfully Yours,
Theodore

Robes of the Gods

§ *for Stefan Hirsch, 1899–1964*
(after his painting "Robes of the Gods")

As the wind discovers itself
through fields of thistle, buckwheat,
great ragweed, like a carefree boy, blowing
his whistle out of a seed, split,
so the gods use us.
           This painting,
garments racked on a line like gaudy,
hung-up slabs of beef, knows this: the gods,
a drone throughout, dress up in brave
and bloody carcasses.
             Still, sly
as they are, loving to lie low, showing
off—a few of us their special finery—only
when they will, they put on the mob
for daily wear:
           jeans, worsteds,
uniforms. But changes they propose here
too, from shrill mad children, newly dipped
skipping in and out, designs-to-be,
to sots, hags, beggars,
             patches
stitched into a motley. And the fitting
wardrobe inbetween, when, stript to nothing
but a skein, hooks-&-eyes the network
of taut veins,
           lovers set off Mars
and Venus, wrapt in one another's arms;
like a battlefield, in the rough and tumble
of a naked bed, the lightning flashes
then, rain, shuddering.
            Attached
to reels we cannot see, impulsive robes

which, brooding, breed, we feel the tugging:
moods our own, yet struggled through
us, rugged, violent.
                    And strange,
affecting wills that much as not resent,
and would resist, the powers investing them,
resent with horror greedy blotches
and the rips
                    the body must sustain
that very moment wills are all knit up
to forward them. By Jove, by God, by bowels
and wounds that Jesus bound him in,
what is this
                    most outrageous dress,
this breath that we spin out, on which
we're spun, the blundering flesh and blood
by which we, living, die, that must
at last be thrown
                    away with us?
And yet at times, although we seem cast
off, days past counting dumped into
a closet crammed with odds-&-ends,
something wakes
                    as though we, nod-
ding, snagged us onto some god passing;
in a steadfast wind, like hides I once saw
drying, golden-airy, in a Pisan sun,
he takes us up.
                    Even as gods, riot-
hearted, drag us, busy muck the highway,
into bedlam, its engrossing frolics enough
to crack our seams, delight bursts
forth that's nameless,
                    whole, inexplicable.
And as they shine through us, like rags,
like slubbered stuff the fire, taking,
flourishes, we shine; through tears
and blood we, whirling, shine.

Sweet Talk

One language surely lets us,
more than another, get at the thing
itself, each other. Attic Greek maybe,
the undraped Sapphic, say, or Provençal,
like honey brimmed on a moistened lip,
when men in speaking felt, so came,
much closer.
          Karl von Frisch,
after some forty-five assiduous years
of "work in the field," assures us
that, did German bees and English
happen on each other, putting up
in the same hive (Germans have
ever been
          notorious travelers),
if one of the Germans found a horde
of nectar, as he communicated this
to his countrymen, the native English
would appreciate at once the treasure's
whereabouts. But would the taste
itself, pleasure
          like pollen,
cling to that fat fellow's buzzings,
in his setting Vermeer-mellow? Might he
not resent betraying his lush secret?
Also, would one nation gladly share
the wealth or readily forsake it
to the other?
          But I've allowed
the slightest, academic hint of honey
to divert me. Language, its capacity,
had been what I was after. So I ask,
Are languages meant for meaning,
some more acquiescent to the will,
the feelings,

and the senses?
Or are they, roughly, equal ways
of stressing? Certainly old lovers,
having tasted all the sweet, so moved
on to the sting beneath, can quarrel
more precisely than mere foreigners.
Wars civil must be
                  the most telling.
Take an artist, working many years
on one small painting or, dissatisfied,
a crowded series. Is it that he means
to be devoted to his primal vision,
often as he wearies unrelenting,
no sleuth hotter
                  on the scent?
Or is he bent on a mystery
he cannot know until the last
stroke, like a sudden period, locks
it in? Or is he desperately responsive
to the moment, inside and out,
submitting to it
                  while he woos
and thereby hoping, if he thinks
of it at all, that the completed work
will somehow, even as it resembles
nothing but itself, be a reality
to the degree that it resembles
nothing but itself?
                  Each sunset,
so we have been told, the day's last
utterance, as well as the peculiar
colloquy of its moment's clouds,
winds, smog (and all the sunsets gone
before?), is unique—recognizable,
believable, because unique.

                Perhaps
speech's primary function is to speak.

The Ultimate Antientropy *

"Unity is plural and at minimum two."
R. BUCKMINSTER FULLER

Whether one paints five Helens
after some much experienced woman
or develops one, his beau ideal,
from the five, most lovely, untouched
virgins of Crotona (such Cicero's
account of Zeuxis' purist practice)
or laboriously patches her together
cheek by jowl out of all the women
he has shuffled through, is not
their end the same?
                So even he
who will not let the name of Helen,
or woman for that matter, be attached
to what he splotches on the canvas,
refusing to be tamed by recognition—
for he claims he paints a painting,
not a landscape, apples, females—
deems he's plucked from out his headlong brain and brush a universal
as it is a most unique,
                    concrete
past any momentary model. And though
we may wish to celebrate the fleeting
or applaud the theory as it lords it
over its bleak and boring product,
Zeus, we recall, laid all (this every
time) his eggs in one small basket;
the consequence, in the most famous
case, was a Helen who inherited
her papa's quality

---

* According to Norbert Wiener and R. Buckminster Fuller, "Man
is the ultimate antientropy."

                most jovial:
being so promiscuous, so radiant-
ly loose, that we have hardly seen
the last of her. The sparks her eyes
shot forth are seeds that will not die.
Men far flung still warm their hands,
their hearts, and more at the thought
of her as at the Troy the flint
of flesh against the tinder of a god
produced.
                Helen, it seems, is more
herself the more she's reproduced.

The Life of . . .

§ for Bill and Dorothy

I

"So there we were stuck
in Alassio all that rotten winter
in a rented house, no one around
but puffed-up Germans, and nothing
to read beyond a pair I can't abide,
Boswell and Johnson, the latter worse
than his crony.
                    And nothing to do
but struggle on through that wretched
Life of . . . . How I loathed it!"

II

"Ah, my friend," I say, "that's what,
more or less, it always comes to,
one book to a customer.

Storms clattering through their lines,
some, if they've the time for it,
wonder how they'll ever learn to follow,
let alone unravel, their chaotic plot.

Others, it's true, are luckier:
richer text, with pictures, colored,
every second page and gilt-edged, bound
in buckram that's the latest rage.

But each of us, like it or not,
is stuck in his own Alassio, waiting
there, flopped open."

III

"Actually,"
my friend's wife now breaks in, "after

39

the first two summer months, after
the Germans left, the gaudy decorations
nailed up on the shops for them
pulled down,
    and the Italians
gradually appearing, rotten winter
and all, we grew to love the town,
admit it.
    Why, whatever the weather's
ludicrous fits, just our garden alone,
with its crazy, tangled, nonstop blooming—
  roses, geraniums, and the rest—
through shattered bottles, cans, and every
kind of litter.
    Or those narrow, dark,
malarial streets at the end of which,
on our long walks, the sea glittered
like a blaze burst through a tunnel.

And that's not all. Have you forgotten
the forlorn little fishing-fleet going out
each night as we went to bed and, at dawn,
returning as we woke,
    threw open
the shutters, and watched behind it
a red heaped up on the creamy water,
the sun rising, as though, towed
in, part of the catch?
    And a bit later
too, once we learned our way around,
the mountain that we loved to climb,
looming over the town and high enough
with its paths twisting to the top
so that one seemed to see—
    a new day
previewed there, just as it was forging
forth—eye to eye with the moon."

The Life of . . . (*Cont.*)

§ *for Irma*

the poem is speaking

"Since, after one quick look,
another friend of yours dared say,
'This poem seems to need some resolution,'
I, a kind of Party of the Fourth Part,
stand up to insist
                    the poem is
satisfactory. Some lines—the eyewash
about a new day, etc.—are a little hard
to swallow. But at least you resisted
gab of chariots,
                    Apollo and his
nags chafing at the bit and all that.
Even if you couldn't, as ever, withstand
your blather about books. What's more,
one whiff of Germans
                    and off
you go like an old horse to a blaze.
OK, don't blow up. I know you deserve
some praise (living through so much
revision, I had almost forgot)

for blotting verses in Part II
after 'each . . . flopped open.' Lines
about people like books, suddenly hurled
across the room, 'with dozens pulped
or fed into a roaring fire
                    that . . .
at last the words all crackle.' Sure
the title fits, just right with its dots,

neat X's marking the uncertain spot,
for those millions
                    razed in smoke.
In any case, I am here to offer exegesis:
like the trio in the poem depending on
one another as their talk composes
it or, ever stuck
                    in their high-
wire act and in the hazy air of new-
comers to the show, the pair your friend
abhors, you stand on them (so you
and your woman spin
                    through space
with no rope, no net, and least of all
trapeze beyond each other). As I now do,
the latest overlooker, telling you
how much you supervise
                    the rest.
And it continues, like the shuffling
pages of the sea that in different light
(and by the lights of him who looks)
look differently."

Between the Lines

§ *for Emily Dickinson*

You, alive, as though you knew
the outrageous fire shuttered away
in you, if taken straight, most stark
when being most elate, must shrivel
its beholder, rarely put yourself
on view. Yet latecomers, prying
into your lines, are dead set
on finding you out.
                    But I doubt
somehow that you would mind.
Like a star that's left and left
its light, grown stronger, gathering
as it travels, as it has the space
of dark and time to swell out in,
you might smile at seeing them
asquint to read you
                    by the radiance
you owned. Sly motes like butterflies,
your glancing words light on them,
then flit away before their hands
can clutch. And still they feel
the warm, the buoyant rainbow-wind
those wings fan up, feel shadows
wading by
                    inside them of a greater
(for its being so elusive) light.
And you will never give them
what they want and so they want
it more. And so they're almost
satisfied. And so are you who long
ago discovered how to live, enormously,
containedly, between the lines.

Far Out, Far In

What we go out for
we often do not know,
though some are lucky
thinking that they do,

like those priests
in their white cassocks
diving into the canals
of Venice after the cross,

or those explorers
plunged, perverse enough,
through swamps and jungles,
most at home when lost,

and those luckiest
of all perhaps, gone out
simply for the pleasure—
limbs set, mind—of going,

as from this beach
a stand of grown pines
closes in, protected past
that by a mountain range.

II

On stilt-like poles
nets, dangling, shimmer
in the wind coral-crimson,
minnow-golden, seaweed-

green—in the fish
one wishes to lure one

44

must anticipate varieties
of taste; nearby glass

knobs for floaters
that craze the sunlight;
also mats adazzle with
fish laid out to dry;

and boats in whose
high-pooped shade men,
women and children sort
the day's many-sided catch.

III

But now, newspapers
spread out on the ground,
rainbow awnings strung
up from the trees,

the picnic, a festival
of swimming, begins;
food taken, some half
awash in the frothy surf,

a few, up to their chins,
go through the motions
of swimming, their arms
a lazy mimic of the waves.

IV

But there, far out,
near the bigger, seagoing
fishing-boats at anchor,
one ambitious swimmer

shows off her skill.
Hair flashing as the sun
catches, already low,
on arms as on the water,

fish dart to her
and as if excited by her
presence, her performance—
no less than their habit

at this hour—frolic,
in pairs, sometimes
in schools that seem one
rainbowed curve, leap high

v

into the air. Then
even as the day goes
down, sinking somewhere,
a glittering treasure,

at the bottom
of the sea, the swimmer,
done with swimming,
by some artful strokes,

sure of herself
as of her course, returns
to shore. Whatever she
was after, as she stands,

dripping yet serene,
a last reflection, on
the sand, she has, for
a time at least, found it.

VI

So, night glinting
round in mottled waves,
two, swum far out, far in,
through one another's arms,

desire briefly routed,
drift upon the moon-
lit current before sleep.
And as the mind goes out,

exploring memories,
sensations like deposits
in the veins, the far-
out, lively places where

the body's lain, elations
gather, sun and wind
and water freshened, able
so, intrepid, to remain.

Lines for an Ending

§ *for Joseph Frank*

Now this letter is on its own,
catching at me at unexpected times
like a kite high in the sky, torn
loose from its tether (or is it
a wing blading the sun?), like
a single patch of snow in a bush
that seems at last to be struggling
free of a long, involved affair
with winter.
        Once a flock of soft-
fleeced yearlings paused to pasture
in its lines. And for a sudden wind
as of danger, the acrid smell perhaps
of gathering fire, panic took
them. Or at times an intense calm
would settle on them, and as though
to a shepherd's pipe they would troop
in a docile order
             to lap at
a lucid pool in the letter's center
or cluster round an altar for one
of the seasons' rites, winter to be
sacrificed to and fed. One by one
no doubt and then in numbers,
pounced on by a passing, ravenous
wolf or harried by neglect, the flock
diminished.
        Now this letter lies,
a ghost, in my hand. I open its dry,
rasping pages like faded, sighing
leaves, and a wistfulness stirs

as in a temple whose sanctuary
is long deserted, whose spaces echo
with lean, empty winds. What troubles
most is forgetting, the poignancy
of passions once everlasting.

The Way It Works Out

How shall I say it
the way it works out?
Sometimes like a bug one gets
stuck in a dark seems all.

But then stepped
back—a breeze maybe
distracts—he sees how big
the world is,

there traveling
together side by side,
a storm and a day,
the two barely enough
to fill his country.
                    This
for a second at least before he
plunges back into himself,
lost like a bug.

II

Haven't you seen
how many make the most—
draggling back and forth,
back and forth,
                    they chart it,
count each grayish twig,
respond to every tiny gust
and glimmer—
of their grief?

III

Yes, we had
covered all those miles,

50

landscapes whirling by—in one day
we whipped through three states—
like somebody's pinwheel.

And there we were,
smack in the middle of a two-bit,
dusty Indian village, wondering
why we'd ever thought to come,
how we'd ever get home.

And suddenly
in a pack nine little kids,
brown as the earth, risen up
around us, grabbing our hands,
with cries drag us out
to a stubbly field, one limp cow
by, to play football!

A Sow's Ear

And for our time
a mushroom cloud to temple all
in rapt devotion, like Elijah
in a whirlwind, heaven bound?

I

Talk about killing. In a life,
translated into chickens, how many
chickens? Enough to stock each chicken
coop in Princeton for at least three
seconds or a tick maybe of all New
Jersey.
          As for cows, how many cows?
A herd to shepherd the assorted grass,
the mooing too, Nebraska requires
on a fine, sunny day.
                        And sheep
with frisky lambs abounding as they
crisply turn upon the spit. Fish also,
and like the others first dressed up,
sizzling out in luscious smells,
then hurtled
                over your flashing water-
fall of teeth, the gullet gulping,
down the canal. All, churning,
turned into one small body.

II

                        Body
of you, one and only heaven I have,
would have, no angel in its snowy down
of singing wings more comely or so
gifted to enhouse and ease me.
                              So you
rightly think your skin the paper

52

walls the world, whatever its twirling,
you the room
           in which its mysteries,
sweet and juicy, are unfurled, spleen,
guts, and day-dreams of a violence
converts the violence into song.

III

So it was when towns out as on holiday,
rags shoulder to shoulder with jewels
and furry robes scenting every step,
dragged whole forests along,
                        haled
in mountains, dug up by their roots,
a sow's ear soothed to hear—its melody—
the grating of the axle-trees,
                        the body
of Notre Dame rumbling in the carts,
the forges ringing, belching spark-
lit smoke that thickened as it mixed
with savory fumes.
                        Exultantly men,
hammering themselves into slim bronze,
their hearts by way of eyes emblazoning
mosaics of glass, reared generation-
glutted piles.
                        And, for the sun amazed,
their tears and blood, so masoned, beam,
     lakes upright, rugged, corrugated,
           as a crag with gales.

IV

         Call it killing, loving.
So now, standing in this willful ark,
     hanging as from a starkest cliff,
          I feel the heaven-high, dark
          carvings come alive.

v
Outside and in
we are assailed. Fingers surging,
loins convulse, as that ark
does with the cataract
of all ensealed along the walls
they stanchion, burly, battered words.

The cliff beginning to wheel,
we, rushed on by its windy rocks,
are caught among a roaring
tide, processional:
                    not only saints
and martyrs once more jigging
as they bask inside
their fire, lighting up
the gargoyles and the animals,

but loitering in archways,
whores, painted as any stained-
glass window, beggars on stumps, slumped
drunks, the building glaring,
as it rumbles, at itself.

A Midsummer Nightmare

It is the waking . . .

Maybe now it's come to this,
a tale patched out of countless tales
some idiot is blabbering, remote
as it can be from its original.

Bessie, loose at every seam, flaps by,
backed by glossy deer, their glazed
looks fixed into the woods or on those
plastered others, idolized creatures,
in her more or less real frontyard.

We might as well admit that we
at last have come to this—the core
of high-toned stories, of curvetting
lords and ladies, sleek and furred
and fit as cats
            ("cats nothing, rather
flittery tilts of gnats and midges,
courting sun")—
              the stink, the boredom,
nameless under the moment's gilt,
their Maytime-buzzing fame.
                   Are we
not proud to think ourselves the first
to see hell's plenty in a furnished room,
in Helen's charms the fly-blown brow
of Egypt, germs at seethe beteeming her blood's Nile?
                ("We sound, in me
no less than thee, the very base-
string of humility.")

                    Yet still
the race by its ground sense commands
respect enough to make me say—

and if already mutants, they will find
their necessary lingo, fables, place:
no less impressive than the virgin
and the unicorn disporting,
Bessie queens it through her animals—

whatever setting and green, ragged cast
the roles must put up with, the play
goes on.
            Inside the obscene clatter
local voices, silences
colloquial, like little lolling
waves in wallowing storms, hold forth
as ever: cricket, river, mountain-
lofty trees.
            ("You think there is
no havoc here, no looking after
rights, good cheer, of catastrophe?
This giant tribe that troops, so grave,
soft-footed ants like shapes embossed
on urns, with their heroic dead
are laden down.")
            Perhaps the time's
come round once more for trotting out
that graybeard of a musical,
"The Battle with the Centaurs," sung
by an Athenian eunuch to the harp.

Old horseplay never long suppressed—
Cretan, Trojan, or the downy god
flopped, rutting, into slubbered duck—
those shaggy beats, black leather
jacketeers, half man, half roaring

motor, now break up the wedding,
the barely held decorum.
                    We'll none
of that? No lout, a hempen, playing Prince, and no falsetto fumbl-
ing at the strings?
                    O let the muses,
thrice three muses, appropriately
mumbling in a row, dumbfounded,
mow at the birth of poesy
in those unlabored in the brain.

Brief though their toil, their fame,
may be, some ten words, ten days, long,
in all the work not one word apt,
the roles forgot before the play begins,
and still I have respect enough.

The will—whether the Will of Avon
or the Passaic's goose—is here:
muddy the mouth, an ass's frowsy head,
a centaur's cleft and clumsy hoof,
the yearning that is love still blunders
into loveliness.

MOUNT WASHINGTON

Mount Washington

At Mount Washington, in Tuckerman's Ravine,
Thoreau had a bad fall. . . . As he was . . .
getting up . . . he saw for the first time . . .
the Arnica mollis.

EMERSON'S "THOREAU"

Insert 942 of the poet who views
and reviews his work from summer's *aperçu.*
The day had been a day, a genius,
to study out in intimate detail
the earth's sweet, diverse plenitude of June,
itself exactly mirrored in that multiple
response.
      And now, night-lidded, day's so many
ages amaze themselves among their dreams
as dateless snows are adding lofty stories
to Mount Washington,
               the one—"highest
in the NE United States, real quality
for skiing"—friends are urging him, afraid
of heights, to climb.
            Had he not crept on hands
and knees—from childhood up: the thorny bluffs
his gang explored—along La Scala's gallery
while Godunov, mid-career, appointed
like the candelabra, lit in its own pride,
giddied him the more.
            Afraid and, as
a guidebook later told him, rightly so:
"The first effect of standing on the summit
of Mt. Washington is a bewildering
of the senses at the extent and lawlessness
of the spectacle. It is as though we were
looking upon a chaos. The land is tossed
into a tempest."

Inching through the Alps
by train, he felt them, churning, scramble him,
this in their greatest wildness with a logic
of their own, serene for very fervency.

But he has now lived long enough to know
he need not awe himself with icy heights.
Wherever he may be, a full-fledged storm
spreading anonymity, and he is lost.
Or sometimes caught flatfooted on most daily-
seeming ground, the stars at midnight striding
that low street, and there abruptly stirs
a vertigo good as the proudest peak's.

A flower, basking in itself as in sunlight,
let its perch be pinnacle or ditch,
plucked, can instantly unlock the pit,
sprung up, impassioned, slavering, of Dis,
sky plummeting as by that tiny ledge
the body is.
                    And so, his pages crawling
with revisions, queries to himself,
and with his doodles, intricate waystations,
he tries to find a certainty inside
against such dreadful falls.
                    Nor, as he views
his work, is he averse to plying tales
of other travelers who climbed this way.
Kindred especially as they had spent
their lives striving to map part of the course,
map often nothing more than accurate
report of perils, loss, and being lost,
scale map in color of catastrophe,
and yet because they had been here a light,
provisions cached in sudden crevices
along the slope.

INSERT 942

In New Hampshire, crisp
despite mosquito-fretting notions of July,
a full moon close as any fellow New Englander,
the crickets choral in their book of airs
as though a grassy hymnal hummed itself,
the poet thumbs *Ein Bildungsbuch für Kinder*
that his host had brought from Hitler Germany.
The first of its kind, put out in 1796
by a friend of Goethe. A most serious magazine
with tidy drawings of the matter-of-fact
wonders of the world
                      (the sometime text below
now in bookish German and French, now also
in an English never heard on Anglo-
Saxon land or sea).
                 Fish ripple through
his fingers, swum in their own radiance
as in the foamy shoals flipped pages make,
names flickering,
        "mackerel, pickerel, perch."

The poet, squinting, cocks his ear. Might he
not overhear, among the moonlit murmurings
his window frames—the lake, moon-piled, impatient
mica mountain, brimmed into the mirror
by his side—these piebald things?
                      And so
he is amazed as flowers seem to leaf
and, sniffing, laugh through him:
                    nonchalance
in roses, frizzled manes. But others ruffled
as—not to be told from—crinolines.
One roisterous, all ruddy nose, for drinking
its own wine.
               Narcissi, self-absorbed.
And then a twinkling edelweiss atop

its precipice, as though these pages heaped
them up to mount it that it supervise.

Much like that bird of paradise that preens
as it goes teetering through painted eyes,
a fan coquetting.
                    With great moths set off
like sunsets, mazy dreams, a map each one
of the Babylon informing summer
                              moonlight
of this night, a someone blinded as he
looks, gets mixed up in.
                         And choice volcanoes
about to wake, bouquets most artfully
arranged.
          There, bigger, huffier than the rest,
"Vesuvius," with people by, watching
from low balconies.
                     Several bending,
     robes a burnt sienna,
                            especially
now they blend with the poet's studious shadow
     (few pleasures like the looking down on mountains
happily in hand.
                 So only as mists,
roomy as clouds, had cribbed him had he dared
to scale storm-battered Snowdon.
                                 With the ease
of dreams the mists like curtains parting, scapes
dissolving into scapes, some cows float by,
sudden pastel vistas, autumn clearings,
prim as album scenes, the leaves compiling
light upon each other:
                       see that intrepid
mountaineer, S.T.C., but on the top of Skiddaw,
in the vales of Quantock, best in one of many
paper-drifted, frost-at-midnight rooms,

hot on the tracks of Hegel, Schlegel, Schelling,
Fichte, all in turn after the edelweiss, and not in a cloud-cuckoo-talking,
smoke-baroque salon),
                          New Hampshire and
the poet intent on this High German view
(perhaps the eyes look up that once set here,
the scenes, asleep as at the mirror's bottom)
of a medieval dusk,
                          toward others, backed
     by hairpin arches, churches fly-eyed, blinking
     on devotions, assignations, plots too sly
     for any prying,
                          strollers in the wool
     of ripened peach and pollen, volubly browsing
     in a homespun moonlight, someone strumming
     a pandora,
                          as Vesuvius, twitching
in its slumbers, sputtering, snores along.

     Meantime, roused in a lower corner—
                                        the poet
thinks he sees their busy, black-cowled buzzing,
this highlighted by the gnat that perches
next to them, a more than life-sized, glittering
angel, stunned by what they're at—
                          flushed
     on them the luscious vines they, tending, trample,
     and their sheep, well-fleeced, two monks exhort
     a woman, sketchily got up, a touch
     too rosy if offhand.
                          And cheek by jowl
     the mightily scowling "Giant of Ecuador,"
     decked out as noble savages should be.
     Swashbuckled, ruffed,
                          the spitting image he
     of George—so wigged and snuffed as—Washington

65

crossing a replica (the artist's version,
adapted when he scooped it from the Neckar)
    of the Delaware.
                    Foot on the prow
    as though, for all the cakes and floes beside him
    like a glacier's brow, his hand is eloquent-
    ly drawn to plant the Stars and Stripes Forever
    on Mt. Washington.
                        There, hard on the General's heels,
    those fabulous louts, half Indian, half cow-
    boy, trooping in.
                    And blurring with the poplars
(the paper, peering through, as though it were
brown twilight's air and of a forest too,
confused with whatever woods were meant;
nor can this moment's moon make clear how many
voices since, how many tramping feet,
have sounded through.
                    The poet thinks he senses
their retreating and can draw them back
as he divines the future already marching)
    as they did for Burgoyne and his Hessians
    until they fall on them, lined up, a whooping,
    bloody fall, the red coats redder, glinting
    in the sun as in the flash of guns
    and powder-horns.
                    Across the page more apes:
    the four above seem reasonably real;
    the fifth, however—
                        some inbetween, a sport,
        flaunting its cocksure tail much like a fur-
        below and drooping, gold-red locks that look
        a German spoof at newest *haute couture*
        (did not Marquis de Lafayette inject
        a Gallic note into the coonskin war?)—
    "shows itself plainly through the long, thin
    & almost horn-shap'd nose from other apes."

66

The poet knows attention must be paid
even to the unlikely likes of such
as to that daedal kin as well—their amours,
Weltschmerz, rituals, cuisine—that can
not be unless aired in our words:
                              call them
atoms, gnomes, or what you will, the Great
Migration teeming through our dreams, the thicker
they swarm the more invisible they grow,
much like snowflakes confounded in one snow.

So, in reverse, that starry race, the farther
off they are, sped to us from a world—
a book?—that's gone, the homelier they glow.

      Like these "colibri" or hummingbirds whose hover
      held, the wink of snows, dusk wading trees,
      circumfoliates plumage.
                  Particularly one,
    "the Tree-creeper, ivygreen, with a flacat'd,
    trifurcat'd bill."
                In its quiver moonlight
is shaking loose (only a leaf or two
between such slippery seasons)
                the Russian Winter
of 1776 or thereabouts that flocks
like flakes from pages otherwise brown:
sports "of the most belov'd divertisements"
of the Slavic people, viz.:

         "Fig. I,
      The Mountain of Ice,
    wooden scaffolds, about 18 yards high,
    one side a wooden slopeness, cover'd
    with pieces of ice, & sprinkl'd with water,
    on which the lovers, being always numerous,
    or seat'd on little sledges, or standing

on skates, with such violence slide down
that they continue gliding, & for many
miles,"
                    far as the poet's fancy, savoring
this ice, no sherbet sweeter topping autumn
fruits—
        he too, despite his hating heights,
has clambered hand in hand with a companion
up a glassy mountainside, blood tingling,
eyes bedazzled with a noble white
        (who knows whose gazing lightens over them,
        its breath ignited, buoyant, in their breath,
        that crags once more become hot gamboling,
        so paced by them, the Jungfrau passionate),
and then, sledge or skates or no, swooped down—
darts out
            "on the snowy way prepar'd below.

        Such artificial icy mountains are
        every year in the carnival's week with loving
        care construct'd at St. Petersbourg
        [in Peter the Great's wintry Sommergarten
        Mars & Venus long ago deferr'd
        to the Cossack snowpair, sparkling as long days
        & nights they twirl out capers]
                        on or near
        the Newa."
                    Now the poet, certain he
can hear the grapplings, happy first as games,
children tumbling round and round in drifts,
sees lovers' volleys, mixed with others, graved
along the groaning ice of lakes, the years
enrolled in riots, massacres.
                    And still,
        like all the stars in revolution gleaming,
        fires rollicksome puffed cheek to cheek,
        flakes, confetti whirling, dress most savage

winds in furs, the rivers, famines, prinked
out so, stark degradations.
                                    There, just below
the Mountain of Ice, snow huffing like a samovar,
are swaddled folk, selling refreshments,
"a mead of sugar & pepper, to be drunk
with or without milk, & Russian gingerbread."

Is this the spot, the poet wonders, ponder-
ing his page, this point, its dotted line,
to plunk the snow, lugged from childhood up,
that makes the world a mountain-top, a lunar
sight, immutable?
                                    As then, no less,
when through him, like a native shivering
in his tent, a fever roamed that little room,
its wall-flowers, wild through the glaze, maze
quite practical for his hallucinations,
good enough to grace the proudest crag.

This the spot to press the child's first flakes,
memories embalmed in them, the rose
of Chartres not more crystal-clear, or what
a tapestry sought to capture in its spinning:

faces spinning, kindergarten faces,
pouring out to storm him in the playground,
chalky teachers packed within a word,
loves opening like furtive, scribbled notes,
one face among the rest a flowering
that time can only intensify—
                                    the dead,
his mother, harried spirit, freed at last
into the winds; his father, bolted past
the failures of the flesh in one swift hurtling
by horse; and his dear friend, a poet, veteran

mountaineer at least ten years ahead
it made good sense to follow.
                              (Had the heights
        not sprung up, loving and at once available,
        inside his gaze, blue lookings from the snow,
        the piercing sky, as mountains blaze, dawn molten
        down the sides, that time their lives, their vague
        if urgent, lovely fates, loomed over them,
        awaiting their triumphal climb?
                                        So they,
        breathing in their hopes, airs of the much
        loved great, longed for their earthly paradise
        on a forked peak, floating with the stars.

        Yet paradise was almost theirs in knowing
        those, compact of wing and song, also
        depend on them, the moment's topmost mount,
        for being as for exaltation.
                                      This
        in the city man has built and restlessly
        rebuilds, adding lofty stories to,
        nomad as the most desperate heart could wish,
        a wind-swept Alp tossed on itself they wandered
        day and night, admiring its spired
        citadels, its frosty lights,
                                      the range
        spread out far below that he must shoulder
        even as it, dizzying, props him.)
And follow though his friend, having danced
        out on a precipice much like a sparkling
        rapier's edge, plunged into an avalanche
        and now, two decades dead, grows light—
between the pages of this basic book
no one will open, ever find, past mining
itself in some all-giving flower:
                                    voices
ice has locked, climbed out, climb over it

in crocus, lilac, columbine, and clear
the cry the hyacinth remarks.
                              In front,
          as the plate has it, by a line of stands,
          a fur-hatted, fat, mustachioed vendor,
          having already tasted of his wares,
          wildly, a nine-day-wonder astride the world,
          gesticulates.
                         One cocky edelweiss,
     these snows its fathomings—
                              like an Alpine climber
perching on a stock, the poet stalking
via pen onto the slippery hillock
of his creased and tracked-up manuscript,
then out into the air where eagles loiter,
stars in undress, much at home—
                              looks down,
       a summer's *aperçu.*
                         And so the poet
sees that we, whatever crag or ditch
we stand upon, by might of gaiety,
by feeling's cubits, top earth with itself,
its latest blossoming,
                    "Through this," cries edel-
       weiss, the daylight haloed round it, stars
     nearby, "the nights yearslong, the storms and wars
     the world at winter hardly seems sufficient
     for, my unique taste has brewed, brewed me
     my single honey-home!"

SUITE FOR
BORIS PASTERNAK

Originally, at Mrs. Olga Carlisle's suggestion, I translated as faithfully as I could a group of Pasternak poems. And I thought I was done with Pasternak and translating. But then I turned for comparison's sake to already published renderings of his work. And as I read poems past the ones I had attempted, a desire to release the fundamental impulse I felt lurking in a number of them prompted the following suite. Some of its poems, come quickly and easily, depended a good deal on those read; others moved in and out among them; a few used them as springboards. Only one, "Malady," grew directly out of my earlier work with Mrs. Carlisle; once I had finished "Illness" I tried a freer version of it.

A Russian Lesson

Hunched over your pages,
I tighten my eyes as though
I might, through the pitchblack
of this language I don't know,
via the tracks
    you've left
in it, benighted as I am,
by concentration penetrate
the swirling sheets on sheets;
such struggling
    seems just
right, the very core of poetry-
making and something you, sitting
deep inside your Russian
winter, must have understood.

Others, hearing, would scoff,
as your time in its frenzy
hounded you: a grown man, playing
with words no one can understand
while the world is burning!

Oh it was terribly hard on you,
hard as on our Hawthorne say,
hiding away in his mother's house,
scorn noisy in his mind, haunted
by the living
    as by the dead,
the piratical and the proud,
so unbowed by the ruthless fates
they seemed to push them past
themselves

          as into his thoughts
till he was scarcely sure
he had not, like the creatures
he had long pursued, turned
into a ghost and disappeared.

                    II
But I have you to keep me
company; even in my feeling
lost inside this rigid winter's
black-and-white, as through
the reaches
              of time and death
you've gone into, I count
on you. With your old peasant
women, workers, students, countrymen you've come to stay.

The light you shed like a lamp
in a distant room, shadowing
long, frozen lanes, and the light
things cast out of themselves,
glowing in your words,
                        flow
over me. That light reflects
something, a bounty, of forest-
deep firs, lining your house,
snows too,
              falling through them
as through bottomless space,
and in the field across the road
the little cemetery, snug
in blue-bright wooden fences

with zigzag crosses, planted
in the snow, and rose-petaled
paperflowers, children flashing

beyond it as they swish by
on a pond.
                    I count on such gifts,
your great anguish and your loving-
kindness, reaching out, to see
me through, to help me find
you.

                    III
            And this that follows,
a wreath composed of leaves
gathered from your rare garden,
trimmed as I transplant them,
is where we most meet.
                            For
having seen what those who hated
and feared, as well as those
who thought they admired, did
to you,
            catching glimpses of
your sad face through the barbed
wire of translations, I know
that till I try, by giving
whatever love and skill
                        I have,
to let you be in your own poems,
but as they come alive in me
and claim as they release this
larger life,
            you cannot be —
nor I with you—triumphant, free.

Malady

Quicker than the inquisition's night-
sly agents, than the secret police
pounced on you, trussed up, gagging,
this oppression, raging, spirits you away.

A gleam on the night, intent
as watching at your window, while
the ice keeps concentrating. A something
ghostly, fever in furs, the muttering

clock enfleshed, creaks on and on
precisely. Translated into you, the poker
helping and the creepy fire, the many-
dayed, lunatic-raving, all-out blizzard.

The dark like shiny, caked-up ice
lies still. Palings lap the starlight,
creamy among fir-trees, stuck, peeled
sticks, in midnight's fathomless well.

But now the blind snow shuffles
the firs, pawing the air like a cat.
A flickering follows, candles walking,
a phlegmy cough as of a throat long dead.

In this tree-hollow nesting hollows,
sky squinting through, the telegraph
lines, despite the echoing "answer me!,"
as they would spell out phrases sputter.

Twigs and needles gouge all hearing,
the sphere-hung spaces bundle silence.
Perhaps the flickering's the only answer
to someone's frantic "who's there?"

A gleam on the night, intent
as watching at your window, while
the ice keeps concentrating. A something
in furs, cracked record needle-caught.

And biting your lips till they are
white, snow-white, as your face locked
in your hands. Let those come after
read this storm with storms of wonder.

November Late

We've gone through two thirds
of the house by now, and what
we've left behind, a jumble
of junk, we cannot push
back through.
                        Soon the walls
will topple, ashes flying,
and a wind, so inconsolable
there is no arguing with;
it snatches
                        every bit
of breath. And light, just
enough, will rise, a raw-
edged morning like a wound,
to see
                        what wretchedness
is here, what howling
emptiness. Light or not,
who's to tell these chills
from fever?
                        This chatter,
gaunt as hunger's self, grinds
down everything that happens
in its way. The animals,
pulling the holes
                        in after,
whimpering, scrounge and bury
themselves many times over
in rank sleep. The tree
trunks sprawl
                        like timber
gnawed and left by fire
after it has had its fill.
Some hectic, feverish to tear
the world and itself to pieces,
seems about to have its will.

"Fresh Paint"

"Fresh paint?" I took that sign
to be an invitation. Certainly,
clumsy as I was for looking more
closely, it rubbed off on me,

on hands and face and deeper
still, as though my breath
kept brushing it in and freshly,
my eyes also, the lashes stroking

away, as though to paint you
forever, over and over, banked
and stoked beneath these lids,
that sleep shone with the look

of you, the young moon blinking,
darkness too, as soon as you were
gone, the gloom of me, as though,
lightning-struck, it stuck.

Now I shudder to think of new
events, of seasons yet to be
(at best they're fall). All seem
to come to spread that shade,

deep-dyed, relentlessly fresh.
Who'd have thought I was meant—
and eagerly chose—to be the un-
paid sorcerer's apprentice!

Sultry Dawn

In coos a pigeon's measuring
out the morning at your window.
And fallen wash from a broken
line, bedraggled faded sleeves,
some branches sprawl in troughs
and gutters. A haze
and sputter as of a fetid,
snoring breath. Clouds over it,
yet low and luring me
like trinkets in a hawker's tray
or in a fair the prizes passing
of a lottery. And as I watch,
dawn behind them like a washerwoman's ruddy cheeks and breast,
washerwoman too the blather
in the bushes.
            Again I strain
hoping to overhear the song
splashed from your pitcher,
your lips dipped in it, flashing
still, your new-washed glances,
nimble fingers warming as you
wake your nodding mirror.
But the noise instead
as of a brawl burst round,
the rowdy clouds, the blather
in the bushes.
            Oh I wished
with all my might the racket
stop and sleep at least return.
The fair was on, the crowds
come rushing. The stink,
the heat is all, the pushing.
In great disgust you have
retreated far behind your shade-
            drawn window.

A Poem Recalled

Even as I dream of home again,
the huddled rooms at dusk grown large
with sadness and with ghostly crowds,
I'm there, taking off my overcoat,

and as I pierce the thin partitions,
no stray beam subtler, binding images,
I find some comfort in the street-
lights ebbing and flowing below.

Again the houses and the trees, sighing
chorally, repeat their common, fragrant
story. And everywhere old hoary winter
sternly busy with her tidying up.

Again at dinner-time the night
swoops down, like gangsters skulking
out of darkened doorways, gypsies, spooks,
to overwhelm the alleys, much confused.

Again, O City, weak as I may feel,
I listen to you and match my phrases
to your smoking, smells and noises,
to your giant building going on.

This way, for the sake of furious days
rushing down on us, I yoke myself to you
that you may know our past by heart,
know me as well, a poem recalled.

Inside the Storm

As I go prowling through room
after room there's no one here
but shadowy twilight and winter,
winter like a prisoner panting,
maddened to escape, clutching
at the drawn-tight curtains.

And below nothing but that shivering
cold, blowing up scraps of paper
and the snow on snow, nothing
but row on row of roofs
and, like a feverish, unblinking
image in a dream, of snow.

The night's hoarfrost reports
in writing large and crackling-clear
the winter storms now hustling up,
conflicts kept on ice in them
and last year's grief, too monstrous
then for us or only one time's air.

Remorse and blame stoke on
and on within my smoky heart.
Still hungry cold, not satisfied
by this, nor by my sighs that
keep an ember burning in my brain,
pulls down the sagging window-frames.

But then the doorway's drape
begins to shake as though with all
that once passed in, passed out
forever. But no, the gust that parts
it like a fervor pure enough to be
the future means you entering.

There you will stand, poised
by the doorway, twilight turning,
winter too, amazed, you in something
white and simple, white and simple
as a snowflake, the last to come
that, topping, stops the snow.

From A to Z

At last you've come, sharing
this same air with me, as near
as our Kiev, leaning, peering in,
a sultry glance, through the window.

Kiev, struggling in its sleep,
its will indomitable, to tear
the stifling, silk-sly collar, falling,
brick by brick, from off its neck.

Kiev, sweating among its leaves,
out at last, larking with the poplars
along its exultant avenues that first
had straggled here, a mob worn-out.

You think and glide like our Dnieper,
sporting greenest paths and groves;
my book sprouted out of secret roots,
day by day you turn up its prize entries.

So now you bid me sit by you,
and totally engrossed, with fixed looks
going over you from A to Z,
I strive to copy you into my book.

A Summer Thunderstorm

Rinsed and flooded, flooded
through and through, the way
a wind is filtered as it blows
across the Hudson and then
through giant trees in clumps
and finally through the corn
at harvest.
       Flooded, rinsed
and cleansed by the summer
thunderstorm, the lightning
gleaming on the rain,
the rain a shuddering white
host of tiny, jagged lightnings,
a mirror's bits,
          the world,
the trees astare, the bushes
crouching, birds with skirts
flipped over their heads.
I felt the negatives developing
at once, as clear as day,
inside the deepest corners

of my mind; mercurial
the light that plays through
me, the sun at best caught
in this night, in waves
a hundred, hundred snapshots
leafed through me. And then
a heady fragrance
          as of wine
pressed from the sodden dust,
the tracks within the grass,
and water spouting at each
gutter, eager to report
what rousing, ravishing events
it's just passed through.

Blithewood

Like surveyors with their shiny, crystal
tools, precision instruments, the rain moved
through this clearing. Now their lines
connect the drooping lilies of the valley.

And dazzle thunders in the mullein's fuzzy ears.
The first dews dangle from their lobes.
Exclusive as ladies of high tone they scorn
to mingle their expensive, far-fetched scents.

As evening tea is clattering in the garden,
the mosquito's sails puffed up with mistiness,
night, relaxed in silky dark among the pansies,
randomly plinking a strung-taut guitar,

the world relents with dusky violets:
years and faces throng the mind. And thoughts.
Each thing the deft surveyors, understanding
fate, reclaim and order for the future.

This Gray Age

Had I known it then, really known,
before I began this wretched scribbling
(my dear friend, older in the business,
even as he was about to leave the stage
forever, did his best to warn me;
but how, caught up in that dream, fame
and its glamor, could I understand him),
known how deadly the lines of passion,
clutching at the throat, would be,

I would most certainly have scorned
all this desperate fiddle, this dressing
up my feelings, I all absorbed, in high-
falutin craft. One fumbles away at first,
hardly aware of the price he has,
in effort as in fevered pain, to pay.

But now the act is done. Instead
of gags and jugglery, glib cleverness
that hogs the stage a moment, this gray
age like Rome, bored with mere sideshows,
wooden daggers, bags of spouting
pig-blood, cries out for the real thing—
that the actor, falling in earnest, die.

When passion is the play, play,
alas, is over, and the one who long
had sought the spotlight, in it at last,
finds to his astonishment that he's
not mouthing art, the phrases he's put
through their measured paces a thousand,
thousand times, but the fatal, final lines
of earth itself, life, destiny unbudgeable.

To Anna Akhmátova

§ *(and to Boris Pasternak, who wrote it first)*

Just thinking of you—such is your power—
spurs me on to find the appropriate words.
Mistakes? Perhaps. But who can call them that
as long as I am faithful to my feelings?

The myriad clatter on the soaking roofs,
the boardwalks' tiptoed, echoing bucolic
harmonize with a certain city emerging
in every verse, in every syllable reverberant.

Despite spring's overwhelming tides,
muddy roads balk passage like your customers.
Crouched over piles of work, the sunset sears;
eyes blear, bloodshot, stitching by a lamp.

You hunger for the openness of Ladoga
and, worn out, hurry to the lake for rest
and change. In vain. The canals smell fusty
as years-locked, dank, bulging closets.

Like a hollow walnut shell the hot wind
frets their waves, the blinking lids as well
of stars, branches, lamp-posts, lights, one
lonely seamstress peering far beyond the bridge.

In unity as in definition eyes,
like objects, vastly differ; yet the sky
at night, scored by the glancing polar gleam,
exerts the purest power, melting fright.

So I conjure up your face, your glance.
Not the image of that pillar of salt inspires

me by which five years ago your meters
fixed our fear of looking back,

but one that lives in all your early work
where bits of unremitting truth prevailed.
Now in everything, like wires shooting sparks,
your poems hum with our precious past.

WUNSCH-ZETTEL

Wunsch-zettel

Oh, no, it is not hard to be alone
the whole year through. Though I at times almost
forget the sound of voices, laughter, alone,
in any true sense, I am not.
                              The seasons
visit; memories. If well attended to,
new crops they bear, surprises like a shoot
that, overnight left out in dew, bursts forth.
Solitudes ripen, silence, from these mighty
days over my woods and waters browsing.

There, you see, behind the house, my mountains
watching, sensitive to every whim
of light; on the other side, the mountain quick-
ening my lake; and, far beyond, the Alps.
To share their presence you think one needs to be
with them?
            I have the good, long winters here
when snows, big at this window, fill, as though—
just like our skiing days—high over my head
they loom, the Jungfrau's summit reached. Great climbers
too we were, my husband a champion,
you know. Then down, earth rushing to embrace,
the body air that through me morning flies.

And made of eyes, peering into this room,
the woods look round, as through my working hours
stride little life and large. They know no fear,
the birds and squirrels, the rabbits and the moles.
One noon, horns sparkling in that sparkling day,
four deer. Bowered among the parent antlers,
the young frisked so the lawn and this bay window,
like a sunbeam flashing, seemed to leap.

But come, let us go upstairs; for there
the study is, an even better view.
My staircase knight a little frightens you?
A creaky ancestor who guards me from night's
mares. Oh I would welcome a sprightly ghost,
but ghosts at best, alas, homebodies are,
by waves unsettled.
                        The carpet came with me.
In its deep quiet one walks as in a park,
and straight into the past unrolling, ever
by me those I love.
                        This is my room.
Hushed, no? A den with moss and rushes lined.
So you see, sitting here, free as I am
to my work and to myself, maybe I—
your visit's kindness I do appreciate—
can make you understand not I from everyone am lost.
                        That top shelf bulging with books?
The garden books I've turned my time into,
best telling how, how long, I've striven for this:
a garden to be implanted in each mind,
with fruits for others, blessed community.

This edelweiss pressed—between the brown leaves
of childhood's *Wilhelm Tell* I keep it—smell
it please.
                        You catch the windy mountain fragrance
clinging to it still? My leaving this house
it recalls for me—in fifteen years the first—
to visit Europe again.
                        To Switzerland
I went, some six weeks of a tiny village:
the world's lost young, war's handiwork, transplanted
as in one proving-bed. Yes, others there were,
children villages American money

began. Quite so. Pestalozzi named,
after the great teacher.
                              Why did I go?
Because of all my work they called on me,
as you do now, to teach them gardening.
Children, think of it, Polish, Russian, Greek,
poured in from everywhere. Looking up to me,
their hunger made them one.
                              No, no lectures.
For so mixed a group, the other teachers
as well, of every land and adult age,
what could one prepare?
                              So then I used
the moment, out of both sleeves magic, and hoped
for the best. Nature, I told them, can be
trusted. Though how they, plucked from the wreck
of Europe, could trust to trust me I do not know.

Starved looks, the Greek children most, fixed on me,
I did what I could. Expression, you know, one tells
by eyes, the upper part of the lid. But those
had saucer eyes, at least as round below,
in each disaster heaped, huge emptiness.
and then on next year's wheat to bid them live!

There in Switzerland those wintry weeks,
high in an attic, peaked its roof among peaks,
cold, alone, a cot, a chest hand-carved,
one candle weaving.
                              By candle I love to work.
To sit near it, before you the night, the whole
great night at once around you, faces leaning,
flowers, to the light. Then all we are,
the selves of dream and wake, together flare.

By candle—in Germany for darkness all we
dared—I wrote my third book. A night unbroken

composing it. In itself gay, though for it
waking hours and my daughters suffered.
Books and buds so pressed their only out-
of-doors while I tried, in vain, to dam
the growing terror. In vain.
                              Midnight knew
no stop. That May the first a fever-glisten,
droves of relatives and friends—my grandmother's "Forget!"—boxed away in vans.

True, time has passed, much time like heavy earth
turned up and piled upon that time. So then,
and in that children's village, living so,
round us nothing but their needs and the good-
natured elements, soon signs of change
like crocus tips in frozen clods peeped through.

Here, let me show you that time's first harvest.
As European young ones used to, for me
they drew a Wunsch-zettel, a Christmas wishing-
list. And think of it, not one of them
had ever seen a garden. Drawings these
of dream desires, flowers they would plant.
All this and this just one week's industry.
These French drawings, such bushy frolic greens,
such candy reds, are best, yes?
                              Already
I had reached them? Havoc still flickering
in their eyes, in their hands earth began
again.
          To see them watching their hands, skills,
hard won, surprised in colors and shapes surprised,
like petals spread to cup the sun molds them.

These—a little cramped and pedantic, no?—
the British children, with no sense of gardens.

Gardens you thought deep-rooted in the English?
Not in these, mostly raised in London,
cockney, the underground their home.

                       Proclaimed
themselves better than the rest, far better
than the Polish, for they had a place
to go back to.

               At the Christmas party we made
with hymns and games, the Britishers, as though
by signal, their caps sideways, rushing in,
started to push the Polish from the room:
"No place you have, none here!"

                    What did I do?
I was not slow to disgrace their fists with shakings.
Then futile I thought. Beside such as my own,
the shame and wretchedness we grown-ups relish,
how could they feel shame?

                Still the faith
my father, no step from the creatures, had
and took as air for granted stayed with me.

Till three I said no single word. My mother
worried, but the tinkling goat-bell father
tied to me soon reassured.

             "That child,"
he smiled, "only when she can put her words
in perfect sentences will speak."

              What other
namings needed I? Clear voices they were,
the animals, wings, petalings, voices
like the sun in heather loud. Each day
I took him to our flower-beds to show
each fragrant task the seedlings were performing.

Then, dew still wet, fists clenched as though inside
a seed I bore the world, I came to him
and, opening, to show the sod I clutched:

"An affection for our fertile earth, dear father,
I have always cherished and will." Amazed
he was, as much as you, and pleased. Later
he learned my sentence had been read to me.
Still that I chose to memorize, no other.

For words, as they first blossomed in our breath
from picture-books, soon wound into my life.
Already cuttings I tried to keep in beds
of pages to look at when the winter came,
though, turning to, I found that while I slept,
wind calling, kindred, they had slipped away.

Stories too, striding through our endless days,
echoed round the garden that the birds
over their chirpings seemed to nod. For her words—
our aunt, loved before the rest—bent over
us, turned all into a fable, the daily
far and lofty, the lofty near, like stately
gowns by ploughs and geese and hayricks twirling.

Even now, as I glance at my curving
path, out of some grand tale jogging here
it seems, with sweeping chestnut plumes like knights
and ladies cantering.
               A dream it is,
mere revery. For little here can imitate
our first house.
              Oh, yes, this one is fine enough.
The past I've done my best to reproduce.
But how compare it with that other's court,
dense orderly rows of chestnut, or the pool
carved curly dolphin flanked?
                    Then I was twelve.
The garden rang with boys, with games and stilts.
At dinner we hung hawthorn wreaths on a poplar,
shaggy colts to wait for us.

To wait!
Like laughter all galloped away. In the dark I woke,
many trembling nights, as though the dark had sickened.
Not all my tears could warm or comfort it,
not though those tears, like bread crumbs waking
in the moonlight, sought to take me back.

Still even now my aunt, and near the fire-
place, in the standing mirror that I keep
by me, appears: the first terrible time
a grown-up cried.
          Her visits had been jaunts,
her wildfire haunting me. Always she came
with flowers that her face, whenever thought of,
loomed a flower among flowers.
          But see, she stands—
far in winter it is—with her back to the fire,
hands thrust away as though she hates their touch,
this body that betrayed her into joy, pride
struggling, my mother turned to console her.
And down her velvet cheeks the tears, spiky
with the fire, glitter.
          "I cry," she cries—
the gates in my first garden clanging shut—
"because crying, as women ever have,
is all I can, as though the ones I cry
from those long gone were little different.
Oh not to Him I cry but that the world
can do without them as though they'd never been."

Reasons enough: her son drowned on an outing,
and just some months before her husband found,
slumped by his manuscript, his hand fixed round
its "finis."
          I could only blame those two
for carelessness to wish those tears on her.
The heartless ways of boys! Men too I saw.

The new wound started up the old, her son
not even killed, as schoolfriends soon would be,
in numbers, we then thought, past tears' accounting.

Nor those more easily wiped out, as we
one summer day might douse a hornet's nest
and listen to the crackling. Our friends,
whole streets and neighborhoods, all rumbled off,
in smoke a moment tracing the wind's design.

And though her husband's dying and her son's
were terrible, I could not know, no more
than she, how comforting they would become.
For theirs not deaths to tear apart the house,
the garden, and the world.
                              Still vastly opening,
deepening, the flowers stood. I sought them
as if the days, the years, in them might ripen.
At sixteen to those much older I taught a garden
class. People shook their heads: "Of such
a noble line and happiest when grubbing
in dirt!" And looked at me as though they thought
out of my fingertips the weeds must sprout.
At eighteen I wrote my first garden book.
Five now, five paper greeneries, behind me.

And they go on. The games still race in them;
like giraffes the stilts lean over ivied walls.

How carefree once we were, free with brook
and sky and bird, the covered bridge, with boys
and girls, joy led, about to skip across
into the meadow where the loaded wagons
creak with summer.
                      Bit by bit the windows
shut. After such as these, my grandmother,
my father, and my aunt, by the very gaiety

they taught overpowering in the pity
they implore, who could reach out for more?

You are right. The dearest faces stay:
the little ones, themselves like candles lit,
the air around me wafting their warm breath.

Surprising then that I worked with those children?
But one must take care how he touches them
lest like powdery flower, butterfly,
the cool blue flame, the fragile breath, be smudged.

Though many scoff, I know what community
beyond mere place and time such efforts mean.
Community: Comenius first and then
a host untold, monks in their monasteries,
Rousseau, and even Goethe, toiled by me,
the rain and sun so bending, no less busy
with me frog and bug.
                              Note that brown drawing
over my desk. Dated 1840 it is.
Precious itself, far more for what it shows:
Friedrich Froebel's venturous first gardens,
in the village of Blankenburg in Thuringia,
with little children playing, tending the beds.
And in the background can you glimpse the steeple
and the housetops overseeing them?
At once Herr Froebel would implant in them
the sense of being a part of the community.

His lovely word, *Kindergarten*, shines.
But his hopes for it, his work? The rose's breath
often in my beds divined his love.
Him and the others, my gardening's choice wreath,
my father at last, my husband, by my side.

My husband, eyes fixed on some far distance—
glinting in them the loftiest, fresh snows—

my hyacinths shaken by his swift passing,
strides toward the mountains.
                                Always he
must go beyond the last peak others dared.
Oh I can understand the need, to plant
a flag, my flowers, and to stand in a place
where no one else has stood, as I my feelings
first, then in a spot least promising,
those children say.
                        How well I can remember
earliest winter dawns, the first wind, sprung
as from my sleep, a mist on it, the pond's
calm breath; and there in its pane, sheet-thin,
as with night's starry back besilvered, first
I was to see myself, the only one,
even as the sun sucked up that pane,
my look, my breath into the air. Oh well
I understand.
                    After that day I never
skied again. That day as ever I heated
water in a pot over a bramble
fire. Returning, pride flushed on him still,
his dip among far crevasses ice-cold,
into my hot, voice ringing out, he'd plunge
to enjoy the burn.
                        The water cools, then turns
to ice. In it no face but frozen crags—
my tears, wherever I looked.
                                Moments that mountain
thawed. Through its briny flood a prow
would jut, grating on new shores.
                                New shores
that wait upon the olive branch restored.
Wherever dark earth is in time I know
flowering can be. In those small villages
again already Froebel was, you might
say, flowering. In no easy way be sure.
Yet overnight pinched faces seemed to lift.

Yes, quickly in the village such circulating
with the fragrant things taught everyone
good cheer. Strength also, what hands can breed.
A humbleness before the mysteries,
nature at its workings past our reach.
And not alone great lightnings, flooded storms.
The smallest, wood-deep bud, only by shades
and butterflies attended, the light hidden
in it already dreaming, loveliness-
to-be, from blossoming is not held back.

And patience as to know not every weed,
some keeping for the flowers water, to be
plucked. Faith too, as after furious hail,
nature calming, a bed can be scooped up,
replanted, healed.
                    One night the Polish beds,
and more completely than a storm could do it,
were destroyed. Complain or cry they did not;
only their faces, of a calm inconsolable,
turned from me. Again I tried; it worked.

At night, after we saw how over us stars
prevail, in darkness best, stories I told them
of famous men, their trials and mighty triumphs
through such trials, read to them from books
savory as the worlds they, born of, bore,
more piercing not the taste of the sassafras root.

From that it was an easy step to move
to gardening in other countries, ranging
from the Zuider Zee, Salt River Valley,
far back as the Hanging Gardens of Babylon,
the Pharaohs and before. At last to Eden,
the Great Grandsire, nodding through the rest.

So human beings in their aspirations
sweetly stay alive. Not only in the stars

do men engrave their names, but artfully
in earth's perennial habits.
                              Think of having
flowering in your garden—as those children
did—at home, indifferent to time,
the proud Narcissi: Horace, John Evelyn,
Sir Watkins' Crew, Franciska Drake, Lord Wellington,
and all the other gallants, ladies, full-
blown in a single bed, broadcasting subtle
messages, their scents, to one another
on each passing breeze.
                              More definite
than we, these flourishers, enrobed in better
than belief. Attended to, new crops
they bear, surprises that, just overnight
left out in dew, burst forth.
                              But should we nod,
weeds overwhelm, the lusts, the greeds, man falls
a quick prey to, through all the growing rampant.

In the middle of the night Germany so,
a world around us crackling. And we fled,
seeking a brandnew garden for my children.

Out of harm I saved this, their first piano,
their earliest lessons, father's music-stand,
those mollusks, gleaming on the table, bent
to their own songs, stronger than iron cities.
But, like sea-rocks imperturbable,
their siren voices always sounding stranger.
Not long my children valued them, the lessons,
the piano, as though, one with the mollusks,
muttering still that lost intolerable world.

And so it goes. My youngest writes to me
in German; though a young lady now, her German
grows, grows daily, worse. Amusing the errors
creeping in from English. This to explain
the few letters she sends.

                    No, I do not mind.
It keeps the little girl she was alive
with me, as in this glass I spy her still.
And spy her more as more and more my girls
depart, as though their growing, women now,
were growing away from me.
                              It may be so;
our first flight may have set the pattern.
One with that early world they seem to be,
a world like ripped-up paper dropped behind,
like bread crumbs scattered many a bird had gobbled
long before my girls could grow enough—
have memories, and in one spot, would house
their senses lighting and their first delights—
to be, whatever the land, secure within
themselves.
                    Well, maybe later they will find
some reassurance—quite so, like those children
in the village—landmarks, in my books,
a home.
                    Meantime? I wait, welcoming them
whenever they'd return. Meantime, I gaze
into the glass.
                    No, not my crystal ball.
But sudden surfacings in it; and sometimes
too, when I look out this window, I am
amazed, as though a stained figure had leaped
into a painting, strange and yet belonging,
the way one shade can rearrange a scene.
Or on the brightest page a shadow strays.

Ah well, the summers thrive, days honeycombs
enhiving all, on woods and waters browsing.

Then, when the world seems a triumphant blaze,
the fanfare of some lavish conqueror,
a loosening sets in, a letting go.

Each day a leaf strews at the tree's foot
till leaves in sighing companies speck sky.

And soon, the winds a blinded swirling like one
lost, the snows months-long as though a wilder-
ness to cross.
        And yet each flake a footprint—
his who sought to climb to the end of snows?
So lost, their end he may have shared, to melt
into the skies.
        The summers through him—
the gaze of—rise once more, a hyacinth,
as this one on my desk, with his last cry,
ensnared, contracted in a crooked streak.

But how can I release, as out of books
this sprig of edelweiss, the loved ones spelled
in leaf and reed and flower? Say how much
can one preserve or smuggle through in leaves,
stamped with all one's love and grief, cuttings
kept against the cold?
        Never to come
again, not though I plant and nurse ten thousand,
thousand hyacinths, spill all my care
upon small growing things.
        Why one could slash
through all of them and still not reach the dear ones
they are living on.
        You may be right.
By being themselves and nothing but themselves,
to our outlandish deeds impervious,
things make, and cleanly, our lives possible.

Five years ago I visited in Germany once more,
an old schoolfriend most ill. The hospital,
a huge new metal block, stood in rubble.
At her window I saw, and all alone,

a tree. And instantly by the bole's slant
as by the twist of the branches spilling shadows
over the wall, I knew: the slender poplar
of the limb on which we used to hang our wreaths.

After fifty years all that remains
of my first garden. The fine, spacious court
now one bristle of geometric lines,
like those black ledgers father used to keep,
figures—gardens too, he, smiling, said—
I could not follow.
                        No, I'll not go back,
not though you ask me to carry on my work.
Froebel would understand, and Goethe more,
seeing what they had striven for so lost,
Germany, the whole of Europe, changed.
Of refugees, uprooted ones, alas,
there is no end. Nor place to hide the grief.
The birds' sweet cries ensnarled with other cries,
that soil for countless churnings, burials
on burials, too spent to bear new crops.

Here? Nothing so close, so tangled with
beginnings, nor so glutted yet with ends.

New gardens? During the war far as my lake
I plotted land. But the war itself engrossed me.
And after I gave over, let nature take
its own set course. Plants only in the house.
As much as I can tend.
                        But now, the sun
descending, we are come to my favorite part
of the day. Above the lake twilight, gathering,
brims, the mountains as at birth.
                        How good
of you to say from out the children's drawings
the colors seem to flow.

                              Over the mountains
the woods have crept, and like the dusk they sweep
to cover scars. And let them sweep. No, no,
I'll not go back lest scars, discovering
new strength, like hungry mouths ask more of me
than I can bear.
                         One never knows, I know,
from what surprising source, this hyacinth say,
deep cradled in its petals, sorrow springs,
wayward as our joys.
                         One night—if night
it could be called, for the late summer sun
had been so strong it had beglimmered thickest
shades and brought in after-dark a rush
of voices, wings, loud wagglings round a candle—
at my door a sudden clattering.
                                      There,
as out of earth, ice-bolted earth, pawed free,
forelegs uprearing, mouth enfrothed, a horse.

Maned with midday blossoms, is it winter,
dark, denied and roused from its stiff bed
of snows on snows, my childhood mount, chafing
on this moment's peak at being lost,
yet come for me at flood?